YEATS

Designed by Tony and Penny Mills

YEATS

This edition published and distributed by Tara, 1999

Tara is an imprint of Parragon

Parragon
Queen Street House
4 Queen Street
Bath BA1 1HE

Produced by Magpie Books, an imprint of
Robinson Publishing Ltd, London

This collection © Parragon 1999
Copyright by Michael Yeats

ISBN 1 90287 903 1

A copy of the British Library Cataloguing-in-Publication Data is
available from the British Library

Printed in China

ACKNOWLEDGEMENTS

Pictures on pages 5, 23, 39 and 53 and 54 were very kindly
supplied by Celia Haddon; and that on p 45 by
Mr Paul O'Hanlon.
We have been unable to trace the owners of certain copyrights and
beg forgiveness of anyone whose rights have been overlooked.

CONTENTS

INTRODUCTION

William Butler Yeats was born in Dublin in 1865, the son of a painter. He studied art for three years as a young man before realizing the strength of his poetic power and deciding to devote his life to literature. Inspired by the Gaelic movement, he founded Irish literary societies, first in London, then in Dublin, where he returned to create an Irish national theatre with the help of Lady Gregory, the owner of Coole Park. He wrote several plays with Irish themes, which were produced at the Abbey Theatre. Throughout his life Yeats spoke for Irish culture and independence (though he feared the anarchy that might accompany so radical a change), and when the Irish state was founded he was chosen as a senator. It is, though, of course, through the magic of his lyric poetry that he speaks to us today.

he gives his beloved
certain rhymes

Fasten your hair with a golden pin,
And bind up every wandering tress;
I bade my heart build these poor rhymes:
It worked at them, day out, day in,
Building a sorrowful loveliness
Out of the battles of old times.

You need but lift a pearl-pale hand,
And bind up your long hair and sigh;
And all men's hearts must burn and beat;
And candle-like foam on the dim sand,
And stars climbing the dew-dropping sky,
Live but to light your passing feet.

the lake isle of innisfree

I will arise and go now, and go to Innisfree,
And a small cabin build there, of clay and
    wattles made:
Nine bean-rows will I have there, a hive
    for the honey bee,
And live alone in the bee-loud glade.

And I shall have some peace there, for
    peace comes dropping slow,
Dropping from the veils of the morning to
    where the cricket sings;
There midnight's all a glimmer, and noon
    a purple glow,
And evening full of the linnet's wings.

I will arise and go now, for always night
    and day
I hear lake water lapping with low sounds
    by the shore;
While I stand on the roadway, or on the
    pavements grey,
I hear it in the deep heart's core.

to a child dancing
in the wind

Dance there upon the shore;
What need have you to care
For wind or water's roar?
And tumble out your hair
That the salt drops have wet;
Being young you have not known
The fool's triumph, nor yet
Love lost as soon as won,
Nor the best labourer dead
And all the sheaves to bind,
What need have you to dread
The monstrous crying of wind?

the wild swans at coole

The trees are in their autumn beauty,
The woodland paths are dry,
Under the October twilight the water
Mirrors a still sky;
Upon the brimming water among the stones
Are nine-and-fifty swans.

The nineteenth autumn has come upon me
Since I first made my count;
I saw, before I had well finished,
All suddenly mount
And scatter wheeling in great broken rings
Upon their clamorous wings.

I have looked upon those brilliant creatures,
And now my heart is sore.
All's changed since I, hearing at twilight,
The first time on this shore,
The bell beat of their wings above my head,
Trod with a lighter tread.

Unwearied still, lover by lover,
They paddle in the cold
Companionable streams or climb the air;
Their hearts have not grown old;
Passion or conquest, wander where they will,
Attend upon them still.

But now they drift on the still water,
Mysterious, beautiful,
Among what rushes will they build,
By what lake's edge or pool
Delight men's eyes when I awake some day
To find they have flown away?

An Irish Airman Foresees His Death

I know that I shall meet my fate
Somewhere among the clouds above;
Those that I fight I do not hate,
Those that I guard I do not love;
My country is Kiltartan Cross,
My countrymen Kiltartan's poor,
No likely end could bring them loss
Or leave them happier than before.
Nor law, nor duty bade me fight,
Nor public men, nor cheering crowds,
A lonely impulse of delight
Drove to this tumult in the clouds;
I balanced all, brought all to mind,
The years to come seemed waste of breath,
A waste of breath the years behind
In balance with this life, this death.

a cradle song

The angels are stooping
Above your bed;
They weary of trooping
With the whimpering dead.

God's laughing in Heaven
To see you so good;
The Sailing Seven
Are gay with His mood.

I sigh that kiss you,
For I must own
That I shall miss you
When you have grown.

from
IN MEMORY OF MAJOR
ROBERT GREGORY

I

Now that we're almost settled in our house
I'll name the friends that cannot sup with us
Beside a fire of turf in th' ancient tower,
And having talked to some late hour
Climb up the narrow winding stair to bed:
Discoverers of forgotten truth
Or mere companions of my youth,
All, all are in my thoughts to-night being dead.

II

Always we'd have the new friend meet the old
And we are hurt if either friend seem cold,
And there is salt to lengthen out the smart
In the affections of our heart,
And quarrels are blown up upon that head;
But not a friend that I would bring
This night can set us quarrelling,
For all that come into my mind are dead.

*****

The following verses are about Major Gregory

VII

For all things the delighted eye now sees
Were loved by him, the old storm-broken trees
That cast their shadows upon road and bridge;
The tower set on the stream's edge;
The ford where drinking cattle make a stir
Nightly, and startled by that sound
The water-hen must change her ground;
He might have been your heartiest welcomer.

VIII

When with the Galway foxhounds he would ride
From Castle Taylor to the Roxborough side
Or Esserkelly plain, few kept his pace;
At Mooneen he had leaped a place
So perilous that half the astonished meet
Had shut their eyes; and where was it
He rode a race without a bit?
And yet his mind outran the horses' feet.

*****

X

What other could so well have counselled us
In all lovely intricacies of a house
As he that practised or that understood
All work in metal or in wood,
In moulded plaster or in carven stone?
Soldier, scholar, horseman, he,
And all he did done perfectly
As though he had but that one trade alone.

XI

Some burn damp faggots, others may consume
The entire combustible world in one small room
As though dried straw, and if we turn about
The bare chimney is gone black out
Because the work had finished in that flare.
Soldier, scholar, horseman, he,
As 'twere all life's epitome.
What made us dream that he could comb
        grey hair?

men improve
with the years

I am worn out with dreams;
A weather-worn, marble triton
Among the streams;
And all day long I look
Upon this lady's beauty
As though I had found in a book
A pictured beauty,
Pleased to have filled the eyes
Or the discerning ears,
Delighted to be but wise,
For men improve with the years;
And yet, and yet,
Is this my dream, or the truth?
O would that we had met
When I had my burning youth!
But I grow old among dreams,
A weather-worn, marble triton
Among the streams.

the pity of love

A pity beyond all telling
Is hid in the heart of love:
The folk who are buying and selling,
The clouds on their journey above,
The cold wet winds ever blowing,
And the shadowy hazel grove
Where mouse-grey waters are flowing,
Threaten the head that I love.

the collar-bone of a hare

Would I could cast a sail on the water
Where many a king has gone
And many a king's daughter,
And alight at the comely trees and the lawn,
The playing upon pipes and the dancing,
And learn that the best thing is
To change my loves while dancing
And pay but a kiss for a kiss.

I would find by the edge of that water
The collar-bone of a hare
Worn thin by the lapping of water,
And pierce it through with a gimlet and stare
At the old bitter world where they marry in
    churches,
And laugh over the untroubled water
At all who marry in churches,
Through the white thin bone of a hare.

from
on woman

May God be praised for woman
That gives up all her mind,
A man may find in no man
A friendship of her kind
That covers all he has brought
As with her flesh and bone,
Nor quarrels with a thought
Because it is not her own.

from
broken dreams

There is grey in your hair.
Young men no longer suddenly catch their
    breath
When you are passing;
But maybe some old gaffer mutters a blessing
Because it was your prayer
Recovered him upon the bed of death.

For your sole sake – that all heart's ache have
    known,
And given to others all heart's ache,
From meagre girlhood's putting on
Burdensome beauty – for your sole sake
Heaven has put away the stroke of her doom,
So great her portion in that peace you make
By merely walking in a room.

The last stroke of midnight dies.
All day in the one chair
From dream to dream and rhyme to rhyme
    I have ranged
In rambling talk with an image of air:
Vague memories, nothing but memories.

the falling of the leaves

Autumn is over the long leaves that love us,
And over the mice in the barley sheaves;
Yellow the leaves of the rowan above us,
And yellow the wet wild-strawberry leaves.

The hour of the waning of love has beset us,
And weary and worn are our sad souls now;
Let us part, ere the season of passion
    forget us,
With a kiss and a tear on thy drooping brow.

the dawn

I would be ignorant as the dawn
That has looked down
On that old queen measuring a town
With the pin of a brooch,
Or on the withered men that saw
From their pedantic Babylon
The careless planets in their courses,
The stars fade out where the moon comes,
And took their tablets and did sums;
I would be ignorant as the dawn
That merely stood, rocking the glittering coach
Above the cloudy shoulders of the horses;
I would be — for no knowledge is worth
    a straw —
Ignorant and wanton as the dawn.

when you are old

When you are old and grey and full of sleep,
And nodding by the fire, take down this book,
And slowly read, and dream of the soft look
Your eyes had once, and of their shadows deep;

How many loved your moments of glad grace,
And loved your beauty with love false or true,
But one man loved the pilgrim soul in you,
And loved the sorrows of your changing face;

And bending down beside the glowing bars,
Murmur, a little sadly, how Love fled
And paced upon the mountains overhead
And hid his face amid a crowd of stars.

hB wishes for the cloths of heaven

Had I the heavens' embroidered
    cloths,
Enwrought with golden and silver
    light,
The blue and the dim and the dark
    cloths
Of night and light and the
    halflight,
I would spread the cloths under
    your feet:
But I, being poor, have only my
    dreams;
I have spread my dreams under
    your feet;
Tread softly because you tread on
    my dreams.

a Drinking Song

Wine comes in at the mouth,
And love comes in at the eye;
That's all we shall know for truth
Before we grow old and die.
I lift the glass to my mouth,
I look at you, and I sigh.

the indian to his love

The island dreams under the dawn
And great boughs drop tranquillity;
The peahens dance on a smooth lawn,
A parrot sways upon a tree,
Raging at his own image in the
   enamelled sea.

Here we will moor out lonely ship
And wander ever with woven hands,
Murmuring softly lip to lip,
Along the grass, along the sands,
Murmuring how far away are the
   unquiet lands:

How we alone of mortals are
Hid under quiet boughs apart,
While our love grows an Indian star,
A meteor of the burning heart,
One with the tide that gleams, the wings
   that gleam and dart,

The heavy boughs, the burnished dove
That moans and sighs a hundred days:
How when we die our shades will rove,
When eve has hushed the feathered ways,
With vapoury footsole by the water's
  drowsy blaze.

down by
the salley gardens

Down by the salley gardens my love and I
    did meet;
She passed the salley gardens with little
    snow-white feet.
She bid me take love easy, as the leaves grow
    on the tree;
But I, being young and foolish, with her
    would not agree.

In a field by the river my love and I did stand,
And on my leaning shoulder she laid her
    snow-white hand.
She bid me take life easy, as the grass grows on
    the weirs;
But I was young and foolish, and now am
    full of tears.

a dream of death

I dreamed that one had died in a strange place
Near no accustomed hand;
And they had nailed the boards above her face,
The peasants of that land,
Wondering to lay her in that solitude,
And raised above her mound
A cross they had made out of two bits of
    wood,
And planted cypress round;
And left her to the indifferent stars above
Until I carved these words.
She was more beautiful than thy first love,
But now lies under boards.

the white birds

I would that we were, my beloved, white birds
   on the foam of the sea!
We tire of the flame of the meteor, before it can
   fade and flee;
And the flame of the blue star of twilight, hung
   low on the rim of the sky,
Has awaked in our hearts, my beloved, a sadness
   that may not die.

A weariness comes from those dreamers, dew-
   dabbled, the lily and rose;
Ah, dream not of them, my beloved, the flame
   of the meteor that goes,
Or the flame of the blue star that lingers hung
   low in the fall of the dew:
For I would we were changed to white birds on
   the wandering foam: I and you!

I am haunted by numberless islands, and many a
    Danaan shore,
Where Time would surely forget us, and
    Sorrow come near us no more;
Soon far from the rose and the lily and fret of
    the flames would we be,
Were we only white birds, my beloved, buoyed
    out on the foam of the sea!

from
the stolen child

Where the wave of moonlight glosses
The dim grey sands with light,
Far off by furthest Rosses
We foot it all the night,
Weaving olden dances,
Mingling hands and mingling glances
Till the moon has taken flight;
To and fro we leap
And chase the frothy bubbles,
While the world is full of troubles
And is anxious in its sleep.
Come away, O human child!
To the waters and the wild
With a faery, hand in hand,
For the world's more full of weeping than
    you can understand.

Away with us he's going,
The solemn-eyed:
He'll hear no more the lowing
Of the calves on the warm hillside
Or the kettle on the hob
Sing peace into his breast,
Or see the brown mice bob
Round and round the oatmeal-chest.
For he comes, the human child,
To the waters and the wild
With a faery, hand in hand,
From a world more full of weeping than he can
    understand.

unδer the moon

I have no happiness in dreaming of Brycelinde,
Nor Avalon the grass-green hollow, nor Joyous
    Isle,
Where one found Lancelot crazed and hid him
    for a while;
Nor Uladh, when Naoise had thrown a sail
    upon the wind;
Nor lands that seem too dim to be burdens on
    the heart:
Land-under-Wave, where out of the moon's
    light and the sun's
Seven old sisters wind the threads of the long-
    lived ones,
Land-of-the-Tower, where Aengus has thrown
    the gates apart,
And Wood-of-Wonders, where one kills an ox
    at dawn,
To find it when night falls laid on a golden
    bier.
Therein are many queens like Branwen and
    Guinevere;

And Niamh and Laban and Fand, who could
    change to an otter or fawn,
And the wood-woman, whose lover was
    changed to a blue-eyed hawk;
And whether I go in my dreams by woodland,
    or dun, or shore,
Or on the unpeopled waves with kings to pull
    at the oar,
I hear the harp-string praise them, or hear
    their mournful talk.

Because of something told under the famished
    horn
Of the hunter's moon, that hung between the
    night and the day,
To dream of women whose beauty was folded
    in dismay,
Even in an old story, is a burden not to be
    borne.

43

the meditation of
the old fisherman

You waves, though you dance by my feet like
    children at play,
Though you glow and you glance, though you
    purr and you dart;
In the Junes that were warmer than these are,
    the waves were more gay,
When I was a boy with never a crack in my heart.

The herring are not in the tides as they were of
    old;
My sorrow! for many a creak gave the creel in
    the cart
That carried the take to Sligo town to be sold,
When I was a boy with never a crack in my heart.

And ah, you proud maiden, you are not so fair
    when his oar
Is heard on the water, as they were, the proud
    and apart,
Who paced in the eve by the nets on the
    pebbly shore,
When I was a boy with never a crack in my heart.

the rose of peace

If Michael, leader of God's host
When Heaven and Hell are met,
Looked down on you from Heaven's door-post
He would his deeds forget.

Brooding no more upon God's wars
In his divine homestead,
He would go weave out of the stars
A chaplet for your head.

And all folk seeing him bow down,
And white stars tell your praise,
Would come at last to God's great town,
Led on by gentle ways;

And God would bid His warfare cease,
Saying all things were well;
And softly make a rosy peace,
A peace of Heaven with Hell.

the song of wandering aengus

I went out to the hazel wood,
Because a fire was in my head,
And cut and peeled a hazel wand,
And hooked a berry to a thread;
And when white moths were on the wing,
And moth-like stars were flickering out,
I dropped the berry in a stream
And caught a little silver trout.

When I had laid it on the floor
I went to blow the fire aflame,
But something rustled on the floor,
And some one called me by my name:
It had become a glimmering girl
With apple blossom in her hair
Who called me by my name and ran
And faded through the brightening air.

Though I am old with wandering
Through hollow lands and hilly lands,
I will find out where she has gone,
And kiss her lips and take her hands;
And walk among long dappled grass,
And pluck till time and times are done
The silver apples of the moon,
The golden apples of the sun.

the song of the old mother

I rise in the dawn, and I kneel and blow
Till the seed of the fire flicker and glow;
And then I must scrub and bake and sweep
Till stars are beginning to blink and peep;
And the young lie long and dream in their bed
Of the matching of ribbons for bosom and
    head,
And their day goes over in idleness,
And they sigh if the wind but lift a tress:
While I must work because I am old,
And the seed of the fire gets feeble and cold.

the old men admiring themselves in the water

I heard the old, old men say,
"Everything alters,
And one by one we drop away."
They had hands like claws, and their knees
Were twisted like the old thorn-trees
By the waters.
I heard the old, old men say,
"All that's beautiful drifts away
Like the waters."

a faery song

We who are old, old and gay,
O so old!
Thousands of years, thousands of years,
If all were told:

Give to these children, new from the world,
Silence and love;
And the long dew-dropping hours of the night,
And the stars above:

Give to these children, new from the world,
Rest far from men.
Is anything better, anything better?
Tell us it then:

Us who are old, old and gay,
O so old!
Thousands of years, thousands of years,
If all were told.

he tells of a valley full of lovers

I dreamed that I stood in a valley, and amid
 sighs,
For happy lovers passed two by two where I
 stood;
And I dreamed my lost love came stealthily out
 of the wood
With her cloud-pale eyelids falling on dream-
 dimmed eyes:
I cried in my dream, *O women, bid the young men
 lay*
*Their heads on your knees, and drown their eyes with
 your hair,*
Or remembering hers they will find no other face fair
*Till all the valleys of the world have been withered
 away.*

to a squirrel at
kyle-na-no

Come play with me;
Why should you run
Through the shaking tree
As though I'd a gun
To strike you dead?
When all I would do
Is to scratch your head
And let you go.